Country Explorers

TURKEY

Madeline Donaldson

Lerner Publications Company • Minneapolis

Lerner Publications Company
A division of Lerner Publishing Group, Inc.
241 First Avenue North
Minneapolis, MN 55401 U.S.A.

Website address: www.lernerbooks.com

Library of Congress Cataloging-in-Publication Data

Donaldson, Madeline.
      Turkey / by Madeline Donaldson.
          p.   cm. — (Country explorers)
      Includes index.
      ISBN 978–0–7613–6409–2 (lib. bdg. : alk. paper)
      1. Turkey—Juvenile literature. I. Title.
   DR417.4.D66 2011
   956.1—dc22   2010028716

Manufactured in the United States of America
1 – VI – 12/31/10

Table of Contents

EUROPE

BULGARIA

THRACE

GREECE

Bosporus

Istanbul

Sea of Marmara

AEGEAN SEA

Troy

Izmir

Ephesus

MEDITERRANEAN SEA

Welcome!

We're going to Turkey! Turkey is a bridge between two continents. A small part of Turkey is in Europe. The larger part is in Asia. North of Turkey is the Black Sea. To the west is the Aegean Sea. This sea meets up with the Mediterranean Sea to the south. Greece and Bulgaria border Turkey to the west. East and south of Turkey are Georgia, Armenia, Azerbaijan, Iran, Iraq, and Syria.

The sparkling blue Aegean Sea lies beyond these buildings in western Turkey.

mountains
★ country's capital
• city
∴ ancient ruins

ASIA

BLACK SEA

GEORGIA

ARMENIA

AZERBAIJAN

PONTIC MOUNTAINS

KIZIL RIVER

Hattusas

Ankara ★

ANATOLIAN PLAIN

EUPHRATES RIVER

EASTERN HIGHLANDS

MOUNT
ARARAT

IRAN

TURKEY

CENTRAL
PLATEAU

TUZ LAKE
(DRY)

LAKE
VAN

TAURUS MOUNTAINS

TIGRIS RIVER

Çatalhüyük

Adana

ATATÜRK
LAKE

IRAQ

SYRIA

Turkey

equator

CYPRUS

MILES

0   50   100   150

0   100   200

KILOMETERS

Two Parts

The European part of Turkey is called Thrace.
It holds the historic city of Istanbul.

Did You Know?

Thrace is a very popular name!
Greece has an area named Thrace.
A large part of Bulgaria is called
Thrace too.

The Galata Bridge
crosses an inlet that
runs through Istanbul.

The Asian part of Turkey is called Anatolia. A narrow waterway known as the Bosporus divides the two parts.

Map Whiz Quiz

Take a look at the map on pages 4 and 5. A map is a drawing or chart of a place. Trace the outline of Turkey on a sheet of paper. Can you find the Black Sea? Mark it with an N for north. Put an S for south on the Mediterranean Sea. Color Turkey green. Be sure to give a different color to the countries around Turkey.

Parts of Anatolia on the Mediterranean Sea have sandy beaches.

7

Lots of Mountains

Tall mountains stand out in eastern Anatolia. The Pontic range borders the Black Sea. The Taurus Mountains stretch in the southeast.

Clouds surround the snowcapped Taurus Mountains.

The Eastern Highlands are rugged. Volcanoes were once active here. A blown-up volcano formed huge Lake Van.

Mount Ararat

Turkey's highest point is Mount Ararat. It rises 16,949 feet (5,166 meters) in the Eastern Highlands. Some think this mountain is where Noah's ark came to rest. Noah's ark is a famous ship from the Bible. It kept a man named Noah safe during a great flood.

Lake Van takes up 1,419 square miles (3,675 square kilometers)!

The Euphrates travels through grass-covered mountains.

Water Inside and Out

Long rivers crisscross Turkey. Two of the most important are the Tigris and the Euphrates. Both start in Turkey's mountains. They then flow south into Syria and Iraq. The Kizil River curves in central Turkey.

The seas around Turkey are major trade routes. The only way to reach the Black Sea is through the Bosporus. This waterway links to the Sea of Marmara. This sea gives way to the Aegean Sea. From the Aegean, ships can get to the Mediterranean. From there, they can sail to the Atlantic Ocean and beyond.

Big Lakes

Turkey has two large natural lakes. Both are in Anatolia. Tuz Lake is in central Turkey. Lake Van is in eastern Turkey. The man-made Ataturk Lake came about from a dam built on the Euphrates.

An oil tanker makes its way along the Bosporus.

Coastal Turkey

Lowlands hug Turkey's long coasts. These areas offer places to grow crops, such as olives, nuts, grapes, figs, and citrus fruits.

A Turkish man harvests grapes from a thick vineyard.

The weather on Turkey's coasts can be very warm in summer.

The coastal areas have a mild climate. Summers can be warm to very hot. Temperatures range between 42°F and 90°F (6°C to 32°C). Winter temperatures drop only into the high 40s°F (7 to 9°C). Snow is a rare event.

Central Turkey

Beyond the mountains and coasts are high or hilly areas. Central Turkey has the Anatolian Plain and the Central Plateau. Farmers graze sheep and goats here. With watering, they can also grow crops.

A farmer tends crops in Cappadocia.

Cappadocia

Cappadocia is in central Turkey. The area has many natural and man-made wonders. Wind has worn away the soft stone to create tall stone towers and caves. People carved out the stone to make dwellings that had many rooms. Some of the homes were underground.

The weather in central and eastern Turkey is harsher than on the coasts. Summers are hot and dry. Winters bring low temperatures and snow.

Earthquakes

Turkey gets a lot of earthquakes. Not all of them cause damage. But some have destroyed entire villages.

Harsh weather poses challenges for people and animals in central Turkey. These sheep look for grass to eat on dry, dirt-covered land.

Long Ago in Turkey

People have been living in Turkey for thousands of years. In ancient times, the area was home to people called Hittites. Greeks and Romans lived in Turkey too.

This library in Turkey was built in ancient times.

16

Ancient ruins still stand throughout Turkey. Çatalhüyük in central Turkey is around nine thousand years old. Hattusas was the Hittite capital. Ephesus and Troy on the Aegean were part of the Greek world.

What's in a Name?

The city of Istanbul has had many names during its long history. The Greeks called it Byzantium. The Romans used Constantinople. For hundreds of years, Constantinople was a major city in the Christian world. Istanbul became the official name in the early 1900s.

People come from around the world to see the Çatalhüyük ruins.

The Turks Arrive

Turkish people came to the area around the year 1000. They were from central Asia. The Turks brought the Islamic religion with them.

One group of Turks, called the Ottoman Turks, took over more than five hundred years ago. Ottoman rulers, called sultans, had total control. They changed the Christian church Hagia Sophia in Istanbul. They made it into an Islamic mosque (house of prayer).

The sultans also built the Blue Mosque in Istanbul.

18

By the early 1900s, Turkish groups were working to win self-rule. An Ottoman army leader named Mustafa Kemal led the way. He set up the Republic of Turkey in 1923. He was the new country's first president. For his leadership, he got the name Atatürk. This name means "father of Turks."

This sculpture of Mustafa Kemal honors the Turkish leader.

Hayatta
en hakiki
mürşid ilim 'ir.

K. ATATÜRK

Becoming Turkey

Atatürk had big plans for Turkey. He wanted the new Turkish republic to leave behind its Ottoman ways. He set aside the rule of the sultans.

Atatürk's plans for Turkey still influence the way the Turkish government is run. Here, government leaders meet in Ankara, the capital of Turkey.

He made sure Turkish boys and girls were able to go to school. He gave women more rights than they had had. He wanted Turks to dress in European clothing. He put in place European laws and the calendar used in Europe.

Young men and women in Turkey go to school together and study together.

Who Are the Turks?

Four out of five people in Turkey are Turkish. Most of the rest are Kurdish.

Three Turkish teens walk down a street in Istanbul.

Smaller groups—including Circassians, Georgians, Arabs, and Armenians—also make their homes in Turkey.

A Kurdish woman poses for a picture with her children.

Old Language, New Alphabet

Turkish is the official language. This language has been around for thousands of years.

Newspapers and magazines written in Turkish are for sale at a newsstand in Bodrum, Turkey.

Atatürk changed the way the language was written. Instead of Arabic lettering, he ordered that the Latin alphabet be used. This alphabet is used in English and other languages.

This sign is written in both English and Turkish. Turkish letters look just like English letters— but sometimes, they include accent marks.

Say It in Turkish!

Hello	Merhaba	mehr-HAH-bah
Good-bye	Gule gule	goo-LAY goo-LAY
Please	Lutfen	LEWT-fehn
Thank you	Tessekkur ederim	TESH-ek-kewr eh-DEHR-eem

Turkish Cities

Most Turks live in cities. Their homes are apartment buildings. By far, the largest city is Istanbul. It is home to about ten million people!

These apartment buildings make cozy homes for many Turkish families.

The capital city of Ankara hosts about four million. Government buildings line its wide streets. Other large cities include the port of Izmir in the west. Adana in the south is known for its factories.

At the Grand Bazaar

Istanbul's Grand Bazaar covers a huge area. Colorful carpets are everywhere in this marketplace. Items made from copper, brass, silver, and gold shine in the sunlight. Clothing made of leather, cotton, or wool is available. Tiles and pottery are for sale too.

The Grand Bazaar is a shopper's paradise!

27

Country Life

About one in four Turks lives in the countryside. Their homes are made of mud or concrete bricks. People raise crops and livestock for their families. They may make extra money by working in the fields on larger farms.

This country home is made of bricks.

Women take care of the children. They also feed chickens and milk cows. Men are in charge of the heavier farmwork. Kids help with chores.

It takes work to keep a Turkish farm running. These farmers are working in a tea field.

Getting Around

Turkey is a mix of old and new. In cities, people get around in cars, taxis, scooters, and buses. For longer trips, they use trains and planes.

People might use cars, buses, or their own two feet to get from place to place in Istanbul.

In the countryside, people might go from place to place in horse-drawn carts. Bicycles take people on short trips.

Bikes take these boys where they need to go.

Family Life

Fathers are the heads of the family in Turkey. Children are well loved. Older family members are respected. Most kids live with their parents until—and even after—they marry.

Adult children in Turkey often live with their parents. That means Turkish children might be raised by their grandparents as well as their mom and dad.

Turks take pride is being good hosts. Visits by friends and family are common. The hosts usually offer guests something to eat and drink.

Family and friends enjoy a meal together.

Let's Eat!

Turkish families enjoy eating together. They usually eat a light breakfast and lunch. Then they gather at the end of the day for the main meal.

A girl sits down for dinner with her mother and grandmother.

Lamb and rice are popular foods. Seafood is common along the coasts. Grilled chunks of lamb on sticks and vegetables in olive oil are also served.

Sweet desserts, such as baklava, round out the main meal. Thick Turkish coffee or sweet tea are common drinks.

Turkish baklava is made from flaky dough, nuts, and honey.

Religion and Holidays

Most Turks follow the Islamic religion. They honor the holy
month of Ramadan. Grown-ups don't eat or drink from sunrise
to sunset. The end of Ramadan is celebrated with a big feast.

Fireworks are part of Republic Day on October 29. On this date, Atatürk set up the Republic of Turkey. Turks also honor the date of Atatürk's death on November 10.

Kids sometimes celebrate Children's Day by waving flags or visiting government buildings. That's because it's said that Atatürk dedicated Turkey to children.

Music and Dance

Many Turkish holidays and festivals include music. Stringed instruments—such as the guitarlike oud, saz, and kanun—are popular. A fiddle called a kemenche comes from the Black Sea area. Players use it in classical and folk music.

A man selling instruments shows how to play the oud.

Drums and tambourines help set up the beat for Turkish dancing. Dancers form lines or circles to perform some of the dances. The beat can be slow or fast.

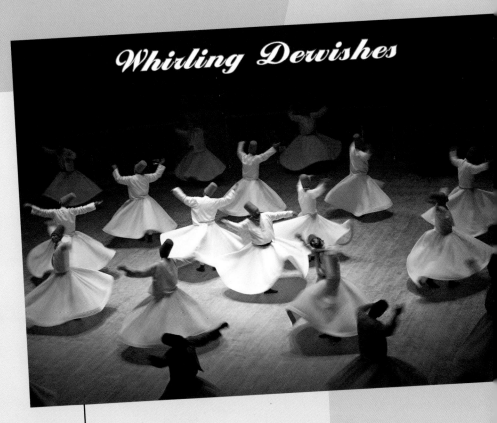

Dear Aunt Mary,
Today we saw a group of Whirling Dervishes. Wow! They spin around and around as part of a religious dance called a sema. They wear white clothing, including a wide skirt. I can't see how they can spin so long and not get dizzy!

See you soon!
Love, Ava

Schooling

Kids in Turkey must go to school for at least eight years. After that, they may go to high school. There they might learn a skill to help them get a job.

Turkish students work on their lessons. These students must wear uniforms to school.

Kids in the countryside often have to balance work and school. They do farm chores or help make goods to sell at local markets.

A girl helps pick cotton in a cotton field.

Sports

Soccer is the most popular sport in Turkey. The national team placed third in the World Cup in 2002. Turkey also has won Olympic gold medals in wrestling and weight lifting.

The players on Turkey's national soccer team are stars!

Greased wrestling is a favorite sport. Players cover themselves in olive oil. They're slippery! An unusual sport is camel wrestling. The animals bump against each other until one gives up and runs away.

Camel wrestling can be funny to watch.

THE FLAG OF TURKEY

Turkey's flag is bright red. It has a five-pointed star and a half moon on it. The half moon is called a crescent. Red stands for the Ottoman Empire. The star and the crescent are symbols of Islam. The flag became official in 1936.

FAST FACTS

FULL COUNTRY NAME: Republic of Turkey

AREA: 300,948 square miles (779,455 square kilometers), or about the size of Texas

MAIN LANDFORMS: the coasts of the Black, Mediterranean, and Aegean seas; the mountains of Pontic and Taurus; the Central Plateau; the Anatolian Plain; the Eastern Highlands

MAJOR RIVERS: Tigris, Euphrates, Kizil

ANIMALS AND THEIR HABITATS: Van cats (Lake Van region); fallow deer, Anatolian leopard (Taurus Mountains); Kangal dog (central Anatolia); bald ibis (eastern Turkey); monk seals (Mediterranean and Aegean coasts)

CAPITAL CITY: Ankara

OFFICIAL LANGUAGE: Turkish

POPULATION: about 74,800,000

GLOSSARY

ancient: very old

capital: the city in a country or state where the government is based

climate: the usual weather in a place

continent: any one of seven large areas of land. The continents are Africa, Antarctica, Asia, Australia, Europe, North America, and South America.

dam: a strong barrier built across a stream or a river to hold back water

goods: things to sell

map: a drawing or chart of all or part of Earth or the sky

mosque: an Islamic place of prayer

mountain: a part of Earth's surface that rises high into the sky

port: a place on the water where boats can dock

sultan: an Ottoman ruler

volcano: an opening in Earth's surface through which hot, melted rock shoots up

TO LEARN MORE

BOOKS

Cornell, Kari, and Nurçay Türkoğlu. *Cooking the Turkish Way.* Minneapolis: Lerner Publications Company, 2004. Find recipes for baklava and more in this easy cookbook.

Demi. *The Hungry Coat: A Tale from Turkey.* New York: Margaret K. McElderry Books, 2004. The Turkish character Nasrettin Hoca entertains with a story about an old coat and a fancy dinner party.

Douglass, Susan L. *Ramadan.* Minneapolis: Millbrook Press, 2004. Learn about the month of Ramadan.

Shields, Sarah. *Turkey.* Washington, DC: National Geographic, 2009. Learn about the culture of Turkey through photos and text in this fun and visual book.

WEBSITES

Enchanted Learning
http://www.enchantedlearning.com/asia/turkey/flag
This site has pages to label and color of Turkey and its flag.

The Mysteries of Çatalhüyük
http://www.smm.org/catal/top.php
This website explores the remains of the ancient Turkish town called Çatalhüyük. The site has activities, tours, mysteries to solve, and more.

Time for Kids
http://www.timeforkids.com/TFK/teachers/aw/ns/main/0,28132,1554552,00.html
This general site has a section on Turkey that includes a quiz, pictures, and a timeline.

INDEX

The images in this book are used with the permission of: © JTB Photo/SuperStock, p. 4; © Brad Walker/SuperStock, p. 6; © Hemis.fr/SuperStock, p. 7; © Eddie Gerald/Alamy, p. 8; © Bruno Morandi/The Image Bank/Getty Images, pp. 9, 10; © Cristian Baitg/Photographer's Choice/Getty Images, p. 11; © Karen Huntt/The Image Bank/Getty Images, p. 12; © Robert Harding Picture Library/SuperStock, pp. 13, 35; © Marc Dozier/Hemis/Photolibrary, p. 14; © Salvator Barki/Flickr/Getty Images, p. 15; © Karl Weatherly/Photodisc/Getty Images, p. 16; © INTERFOTO/Alamy, p. 17; © Richard Connors/Dreamstime.com, p. 18; © Ifeelstock/Dreamstime.com, p. 19; REUTERS/Umit Bektas, p. 20; © Yadid Levy/Alamy, p. 21; © Chryssa Panoussiadou/Panos Pictures, p. 22; © Robert Mackinlay/Peter Arnold Images/Photolibrary, p. 23; © Amer Ghazzal/Art Directors & TRIP, p. 24; © Brian Gibbs/Art Directors & TRIP, p. 25; © Mikhail Nekrasov/Dreamstime.com, p. 26; © Vitaly Titov/Dreamstime.com, p. 27; © David Preutz/Alamy, p. 28; © Yaacov Dagan/Alamy, p. 29; © Mark Henley/Panos Pictures, p. 30; © Ohad Reinhartz/Alamy, p. 31; © Blaine Harrington III/Alamy, p. 32; © Yoray Liberman/Getty Images, pp. 33, 34; © Murat Taner/Photographer's Choice/Getty Images, p. 36; REUTERS/Stringer Turkey, p. 37; © Art Directors & TRIP, p. 38; © Bruno Morandi/Stone/Getty Images, p. 39; © Janine Wiedel Photolibrary/Alamy, p. 40; © Dieter Telemans/Panos Pictures, p. 41; AP Photo/Ibrahim Usta, p. 42; REUTERS/Fatih Saribas, p. 43. Illustrations by © Laura Westlund/Independent Picture Service. Front cover: © Salajean/Dreamstime.com.